What About the Man? Surviving Pregnancy

Matt Perkins

www.whatabouttheman.com
Facebook: WAM-What About the Man?
Twitter: @coachmperkins

Cover by Lou Fister

DEDICATION

This book is dedicated to our North Carolina
friends with whom my wife, Faith, and I
experienced our first three pregnancies.

CONTENTS

ACKNOWLEDGMENTS

I would have no material if my wife had not birthed four children. I thank her for putting up with all my complaining about surviving pregnancy when she was the one truly surviving pregnancy. I thank my children, Isaiah, Alexis, Audrey, and Timothy because without their births and making their mom sick while they were in the womb the book would not have quite the same flavor. A special thanks goes to Lou Fister, who designed and developed the book cover. None of this would happen without Christ giving me the strength to put thoughts to words and without Him guiding me through my work.

PREFACE

Two ideals exist for this book. First, my ultimate goal is for men to read this book and to know they are not alone when it comes to dealing with, I mean, accepting the reality of pregnancy. While some literature on the subject exists, much of it is from a woman's perspective. What? How can a woman tell me how I feel and think about pregnancy? I'm sure women would love it if a man wrote a book about how women feel during pregnancy. Insert a little sarcasm there. And, most literature is hundreds and hundreds of pages long. Why do I need a 500 page book to explain to me what to expect when expecting when "expecting" is a natural thing that billions of people have experienced? Most men don't read that stuff!

On the other hand, women, if you are reading this, either your significant other is trying to help you see perspective, so please be understanding, or you may be reading this because you have some desire, while it may be deeply imbedded in the inner-recesses of your soul, to know what he is/will be experiencing during the pregnancy time period. Whatever the case, please have an open mind. Realize many of the written words are for comedic relief, and while you may disagree with or be offended by my thoughts, they are just that--my thoughts. I would argue most men experience similar feelings as will be shared in the book, but we all have different personalities, experiences, and beliefs that ultimately shape how we experience the whole pregnancy phenomenon.

Finally, please enjoy reading this view of pregnancy from a man's perspective. I am often blunt and sarcastic, so don't read too deeply into everything I write. As we begin this journey together, I realize not all men are in the same circumstance as the typical "expecting" male, but for simplicity sake, this book will be told from my perspective, a married male.

Oh yeah, one more thing: Through my wife's first three pregnancies, I continuously claimed there was a need to write a book, but I never did. Then I left a great education job, moved from our family's home base in North Carolina for the past eight years to live by my wife's family in the cornfields of northeast Ohio, left our best friends, neighbors, and church behind, and moved into my in-laws basement while accepting a part-time job as my wife took a part-time job herself. Our world was rocked, not by force, but by choice. As a man of faith, I believed this was where God wanted us. However, as if that weren't enough challenge, the reality is I could not most effectively write this book from past experiences and through other's pregnancy adventures. So, as a complete surprise, child number four was conceived and this book was birthed!

1

PRE PREGNANCY

I know children bring new, exciting dynamics to marriage, but life before children, and before each pregnancy, reveals freedoms that many males struggle to give up. I married my wife, Faith, when I was twenty-five, and during that first year of marriage, as a couple we had all the freedom to do as we pleased.

One day at the end of the school year, I came home, and Faith said, "Hey, I found awesome plane prices to go to Hawaii!" So, we booked them, and three weeks later we were in Hawaii. On a side note, unfortunately, when I looked back at pictures, I saw first-hand what the first year of marriage had done to me. Hello Shamu! I couldn't believe I took my shirt off on the beach!

If we stayed up late one night or decided to go away for the weekend, who cared? We could find a time to nap or sleep in Saturday and/or Sunday. Whether it was Saturday morning basketball, Friday night or Saturday afternoon football games, or school sporting events throughout the week, I was there.

Likewise, I can remember seeing parents at the store with their young children, holding little Johnny's hand, telling little Sarah to stop running through the clothes, and yelling at two siblings to stop hitting each other. Hey, I just want to go to the store, buy what I need, and go home. I don't want to deal with all that hoopla. As a side note, if you see children at the store act out and throw fits and think to yourself, "My children will never do that," think again. You can't control a one or two-year-old's emotions! What's more, I remember countless plane flights of listening to screaming babies and times in restaurants when parents left their food behind to take the kids to the car for "life changing" consequences. Well, I remember when I was a kid that I was "that child."

Furthermore, think about attending sporting events. I remember seeing dads in the bathroom trying to figure out how to change a child's diaper while suspending the child in the air to avoid the toxic, bacteria plagued facility we call the public restroom. At the same sporting events, as the games go down to the wire, parents are often forced to leave games early to deal with their tired, screaming children.

So, ladies, when men start to get antsy about the possibility of pregnancy, just remember those visions we have and the sounds we hear when we imagine life with children. Men, what you have seen at the store is true, but it is surprising how much you can, and will, endure when you love your children.

I'm here to tell you that while we all have different thoughts about and views of impending pregnancies, no honest man will tell you that he does not feel some sense of loss of freedom. We are wired for adventure! We are wired to make things happen, and the thought of our friends going out Friday night while we are stuck at home on babysitting duty does not sound enticing. In fact, I'd go so far as to say that really, we just don't want to grow up, and children equal responsibility, which equals the need and requirement for us to actually act mature and to be responsible!

Survival Tips:

1)Start paying attention to other parents' parenting skills. Whose kid is respectful, and which ones scream and cry all the time? As I tell my speech students, "Emulate the masters!"
2)If there's still time, savor the kid-free moments!

2

YOU'RE PREGNANT!

The truth is we all have different responses to finding out our wives are pregnant. Let's break things down into a few categories, and, Men, maybe you can figure out what will best match your reaction. Share that with your wife so she knows what to expect. This can save a lot of grief. Women, make sure you know how your man feels about the whole pregnancy thing. We're not necessarily thinking what you're thinking. This may help spare you some tears.

Response 1 - I'm as excited as you! This is the best day of my life!

This response is from the man who's been dreaming about having children before he was married. He may not have experienced much in the world, so he doesn't have much to lose, or maybe he is just excited about the fact that there may be "more" of him in the world. Or, he may truly love children and is just excited to have his own. Whatever the case, you can't go wrong with this response. In fact, Men, you might be having a good night later on! Ladies, if you get this response from him, just go with it and don't second guess it.

Response 2 - That's great! I'm so excited for you!
While on the surface this response sounds affirming and positive, notice the key word in the second statement - *you*. Ummm, you're both supposed to be excited. Chances are if a man gives this response he's also not jumping up and down like the guy in response number one probably is. Men, this response is fine. It is hard for us to admit that life as we know it will no longer be the same. Ladies, just realize we are wired differently from you, and we while we may not show the same excitement, we can still be excited.

Response 3 - Are you sure you're pregnant? Can those tests be wrong?

Ladies, again, don't fret over this response. We don't read all the books and take all those pregnancy tests you hide from us. One line, two lines, blue line, green line--we don't know what those mean. We need assurance and confirmation. Also, while the men with this response usually knew pregnancy could very well "happen," we often reject the fact it will actually happen to us. Just take another test if it will help, or just give us some time. In no time your man will be holding you in his arms, or so you hope.

Response 4 - What do you mean you're pregnant? How did that happen?

Men, if this is your response, you must have missed health class, or you may not be aware of everything in your marriage. Ladies, good luck! Seriously, maybe the reality of pregnancy is all too overwhelming. If this is the case, both parties involved need to be patient with the other. Men, you have got to realize that this is what she wants, we hope, so support her. And if she's as surprised as you, then step up and be there for her. Ladies, if this is the opposite response you're looking for, realize he is just overwhelmed and give him time.

While I'd like to say my response was one of loving tenderness and care, it wasn't. For all four kids, I've found out differently, but the first is the one most people remember. I walked into the bathroom and saw something either on the floor, sink, or trash can. I can't remember; I was too caught off guard. I saw those lines and said, "Faith, what are these? What do they mean?" I don't think I'd seen a test before that. Once she answered my questions, my next response was, "You need to take another one. How do we know it's right?" I'm definitely not the first to respond like that, but what was I thinking? All those test have a 99% failure-proof claim. After I calmed down, I'm pretty sure I hugged my wife and told her how much I loved her and how excited I was. No, I definitely did that. I have no doubt about that. Just don't ask my wife.

If we skip to child number four, we see a different response but with a similar surprised, *What's happening?* attitude. Truthfully, after our third child, Audrey, was born, I was content with being done. Now, while it's my own fault I didn't have anything permanent done to my body, after two years of nothing happening, I thought we were safe. Ha, what was I thinking! And, what's worse, we were living in my in-laws basement, after our move from the sunshine state of North Carolina to the cloud-filled skies of Ohio. Here's how that occurred:

Most men don't look with anticipation for the woman's "time of month" to start. However, as there was nothing else to do while living in the basement, we had to do something so I was constantly nervous about what could happen. Well, the previous month provided a scare as "things" were a week late. However, the following month, Faith started feeling "funny." That could only mean one thing, but I kept thinking about the fact that we would be in the basement for three more months! Well, one night I was tired of hearing about, and thinking about, Faith possibly being pregnant, so I made a quick trip to the store to buy a pregnancy test. I went down to the basement and gave it to Faith. She wanted to wait a little longer, but I knew that wouldn't last and before I knew it she had a present to show me--

the blue lines! Well, I held my composure and lasted two-and-a-half more months in the basement...with a sick, pregnant wife. On the outside I was the picture of the calm, collected pillar of a husband. On the inside, I just saw four more years of college tuition!

Survival Tips:

1)If you're in this state of giving a friend advice, whatever you do, act supportive. Don't make your wife cry tears of fear. Make her feel excited!
2)Plan for the future! If you don't want this to happen, take permanent measures! Trust me, or you may get that extra surprise.

3

LAST CHANCE AT FREEDOM

In chapter 1 I touched on the fact that men often struggle with the reality of having children because we view parenting as creating a loss of freedom. It's not that we don't necessarily want children or that we are too selfish and can't think of anyone but ourselves, or we're too irresponsible to take care of children. Although, let's be honest, at times that can be the case. However, we simply are fearful of losing our freedom.

Freedom - It seems like a simple, easy to define word...not so fast. Countries have wars over freedom, society and teenagers spend years battling for and against freedom, and spouses often times fight for it from the second they say "I Do." We all have our own ideas of what freedom is for us. Many men, including myself, often view the weekend as days of freedom to play sports, attend events, work around the house, or just relax. However, our spouses don't always view it that way. While we think the weekend provides that freedom to hang out with the guys Saturday night, the pregnant wife might think freedom means the opportunity to watch a romantic movie, go shopping for more baby stuff, or talk about baby stuff...all day long.

Men, I strongly advise you to enjoy those nine months of pregnancy for all they are worth. If you already have children, life will be different for you, but if you don't dive in and enjoy. Stay up late when you can. Have those marathon TV and movie watching hours and days with all the video streaming available. Go on those short weekend get-a-ways. Join those rec sports leagues and relive those high school glory sports days! Work out as much as you can because that will take a back seat once children join the family. Those are all fun, extra-curricular activities that don't necessarily go away once children arrive but that are much more difficult to make time for. The reality is that the responsibility of children brings with it a need for more structured time, which in most cases makes it more difficult, but not impossible, to take part in all the activities you enjoy doing.

Likewise, Men, if you have any projects around the house to complete, do them sooner rather than later. When there's one child, there can still be ample time to work on projects as they often nap, but then you're tired from not sleeping enough. And, you will find that if you suddenly have a spurt of energy, your wife won't, and you will be on baby duty while she rests! Chances are that your baby will be crying and won't let you work during those times. Let's be honest, I think there's a conspiracy among the women out there that trains the baby's psyche to know the exact moments to start acting out.

Finally, and thankfully Faith doesn't over-react like many mothers, but for some reason, many women, especially new mothers, think every little chemical smell (paint, cleaners, burnt food, etc.) will harm the baby. Now, I understand that children's bodies are not as developed as ours and that they can negatively react to things, but our society has gone way overboard! My point is, if your wife reads into everything and allows all the media propaganda to think for her rather than think for herself, you will not be allowed to do certain projects with a baby around.

Ladies, I know some of what I've said might incite you, but realize that the whole pregnancy phenomenon hits most men differently from women. Do I know many women miss the freedom of having no children responsibilities? Absolutely! I also know that you are the ones carrying the baby, which takes away from you more than it does us. However, and I can't believe I'm admitting this, but most women are simply more emotionally prepared for parenthood. Women are generally more mature than men when it comes to parenthood, and women usually are much less self-centered than men. So, I know that while parenthood is an awesome responsibility that no one should take for granted, it can still be difficult for both sexes to prepare for.

Survival Tips:

1)Go have some fun! If you don't now, it may be years before you go anywhere with just the two of you.

2)Start planning "Man Night Out" so once the children come you must "carry on the tradition." Encourage your wife to have "women's night out" as well. Trust me, if you give a little she'll give back...hopefully, in more ways than one!

4

SICK, PREGNANT WOMAN

Wow, I mentioned Shamu earlier, but that is nothing compared to what happens to a man during pregnancy, especially with a sick wife. The average man gains ten pounds during pregnancy, so if you thought you were overweight before pregnancy, count on those pants getting even tighter, count on those love handles becoming a little more loving, and count on those moobs (man boobs) coming out full force--all because your wife is pregnant and sick!

Women's bodies all deal with pregnancy in different manners, externally and internally. As a result, not all men experience the pregnancy life in the same manner. However, you need to be on guard because if you are not you will be in for a rude awakening.

External Differences:

Because men are visual, I'm sure we've all looked at pregnant women and thought, "Wow, what did she do wrong to gain all that weight?" or "That woman hasn't gained anything except for that round ball in her stomach." The reality is women's bodies are all different, causing most to gain weight, and some to lose weight, in different manners and fashions.

Fortunately, through her four pregnancies my wife just gained the typical 25-35 pounds, so I consider myself blessed. She has an athletic body and physically looks to be in great shape. However, I can think of a friend who was even smaller than my wife, yet, once pregnancy hit, she started gaining weight just by looking at food. She wasn't even necessarily overeating, but her hormones and metabolism took a beating. Ladies, don't fret, she did return to her pre-pregnancy body, but it takes some work.

At the same time, I've known tiny, petite women and thought to myself, "They are in for it when that pregnancy hits full-on," but they remain tiny and pop out average-sized babies. Where were they storing those babies? On the flip side, I've known and seen overweight ladies become pregnant and lose weight throughout pregnancy. I'm here to tell you that I don't think that's the best way to go about losing weight. I wonder if they blackmailed their husbands and said, "I will lose weight and have sex with you only if you let us have children." Hey, that's not a fair thing to do, by the way.

On a side note, while most women's bodies do get bigger, that's not always a bad thing. Let's remember, men are visual, so you might notice that once plain-looking, V-neck shirt all of the sudden has come to life, and you want her to wear it every day! She may feel uncomfortable with the new "growth" but...I guess we can accept it. I'll save face here and say that when she asks if something is not "appropriate" to wear in public anymore, just be honest with her. You can look later.

You also might note physical changes in your wife other than weight gain. Without going into too much detail, let's just say that lines on her body may start forming where they didn't exist before. This could include stretch lines and a weird line that forms by her naval. In fact her naval may change. Have you ever noticed that belly button protruding through a pregnant woman's shirt? Her hair may change due to hormonal changes in her body, hence the beginning of the "short haircut" syndrome for some. Along with that, you may find more and more of her hair in the bathroom.

Regardless, Men, I encourage you to have no preconceived notions as to what you expect your wives' bodies to look like during, and after, pregnancy. They won't be normal; that's all you need to know. To tie this into sickness, the reality is often times the only thing that cures women's pregnancy sickness is food. So, you must ask yourself, do you want a sick, pregnant woman who's constantly in pain who constantly complains, but still looks hot, or are you willing to sacrifice a momentary lapse on "hotness" and encourage your wife to eat, in order for her to avoid the dreaded sickness?

Internal Differences:

While I mentioned my wife gained average weight during her pregnancies, unfortunately, she was sick through the entire first pregnancy, three quarters of the second pregnancy, and off and on during the third pregnancy. The fourth pregnancy was brutal as Faith was sicker than ever, and we were in the in-laws basement for the first four months. She, and most pregnant women, not only deal with the physical changes, but pregnancy sickness messes with everything inside of them. Hence, it messes with the man!

During Faith's first pregnancy, here's a typical conversation about eating out:

"Hunny, I am craving some Mexican food. Can we go out to a Mexican restaurant?"

"Of course, anything for you." (Maybe I don't always say that.)

We arrive at the restaurant, sit down, and order. The food comes, and here's what comes next:

"Oh, I can't stand the smell of that. I don't want Mexican anymore!"

"Uh, are you sure? We do have to pay for this."

"Yes, it's going to make me sick."

"Well, let's give it a few minutes."

So, I begin eating my food, enjoying it very much, and my wife just looks like she's going to the pit of hell.

"Ok, we'll get a box and take it all home. And then I'll eat not only my food but yours as well so we aren't wasteful." Welcome to the plus ten pounds!

You can give your wife wrist bands that help with seasickness, you can give her a massage, get her new food, etc. Sometimes you just need to leave her alone, and sometimes you just need to let her sleep. Unfortunately, there's no magic answer to "dealing" with, I mean "helping", your sick, pregnant wife. However, for us, Faith finally relented during the fourth pregnancy and took some doctor-prescribed nausea medication. Like magic, it worked!

Now, I realize that many people don't like taking medicine, myself included, as I'm a big proponent of mind over matter. However, empirical evidence doesn't lie. When people with headaches don't take medicine, they walk around in a fog and can contribute little to the world around them. When they take medicine, they join the world and effectively function. Such has been the case with my wife. The first time she took her magic pill for nausea, she was wiped out as drowsiness is often times a side effect of the medicine. However, she felt much better when she was awake. And, as I explained to her, as she gradually took the medicine, her body would accept it better and the side effect would not be as bad. As fate would have it, I was right! A couple of days later when she took it again, her drowsiness was not nearly as bad, and she was functioning on a much higher level and felt much better. Obviously, from my perspective, I'm excited the doctor encouraged her to try the medicine as I now somewhat had my wife back. However, more importantly, for my wife's sake taking the medicine allowed her to feel much better and to want to do something other than sleep the nausea off.

Pregnancy, and having children, requires people to become much less self-absorbed and more selfless. That's a natural phenomenon as people's responsibility and focus of their lives changes with the addition of other beings in their lives. Likewise, while the husband is not "carrying" a child in his womb, he must be that extra support and strength for his wife. Even if pregnant women don't experience the sickness and other issues that my wife and others have faced during pregnancy, they still often need, and deserve, the emotional and physical support of their husbands. From an honest man's standpoint, this can be a lot for us and can be a great challenge as we look at how our lives will be changing. Therefore, the added stresses of a sick wife, a tired wife, and anything else related to pregnancy is a burden for many men. While we must man up and carry that burden and be the pillar our wives need, let's not forget that there are two people going through the pregnancy together!

Survival Tips:

1)Pray, pray, pray for your wife's health. If God answers your prayer by allowing for pregnancy sickness to run its course, make yourself feel better knowing that you obviously are superhuman. Otherwise, God wouldn't give you such a difficult test. If you don't believe in God, do the crazy chicken dance, offer offerings to what or who you believe in, or do whatever it is you do when trying to avoid a crisis.

2)Stock up on your wife's cravings so you don't have to run to the store late at night.

3)Order something small when you eat out. You may be eating most of hers, and she may take two bites and decide she wants something different.

5

FINANCES

Let's be honest, even if you really do have faith that all will be ok by adding children to the financial equation in the house, everyone, in some way shape or form, realizes the financial strain/challenges that children bring to marriage. I realize we live in an era where both men and women have dreams and aspirations of making it big and of having financially rewarding jobs. In many cases, we like those financial rewards as we can spend money on ourselves. Now, I realize I chose a non-financial rewarding profession, and spent ten years teaching in one of the lowest teacher-paying states in the nation, but my wife and I still had money. And because before children we both worked, we had plenty of money to both save and spend.

However, hello baby! I never imagined how expensive having children could be. I thought you just buy them diapers, clothes, and food. Ha, in what fantasy world was I living? My wonderful wife has had no problem with hand-me-downs, and I still feel like we've already paid enough to send one child through college. Unfortunately, many women like new things so get ready! Following is a quick list of things you will be buying for the upcoming birth...and the list just gets bigger when the baby arrives:

1)Stroller/car seat - $100-$500

2)Cribs - $100-$400

3)Matching furniture - $$$

4)Baby clothes - $$$

5)Diapers - at least $30-$50/month

6)Baby Monitor - $100-$300

7)All that "cute, adorable" baby bedding and wall hangings - $100-$300

8)Rocker - $100-$300

9)Exersaucer, boppy (yeah, that's a real thing), bouncy seat, high chair, etc. - $$$

10)Bibs, blankets, spit up cloth (they will spit up), etc. - $100

11)Baby room decorating (painting, shelves, pictures, etc.) - Up to hundreds of $$$'s

The list can go on, but if you even think about buying all that stuff and compare it to buying a new car, there's not much difference. However, you can be saved from spending all that money, but be aware, it could create WWIII in your house. You could use "used" baby stuff. Or, maybe you could consider not getting all that "stuff." Thirty years ago, half of all the modern baby products didn't exist, and we're all fine. (Well, actually, we're not and maybe that's the problem!) I know, some people are cringing at the thought of it. "How could my baby, who can't even see anything but blur marks for the first couple of months, be forced to sleep in an undecorated room?" "How could I use a stroller someone else used? Aren't they unsafe? Don't I need to have all new things because my child will remember all of that when he/she gets older?"

Seriously, get over yourself. Now, I don't want to say never buy or ask for new things. I'm simply saying quit falling into one of the biggest modern day genius marketing ploys. Quit letting your selfishness (yes, we like all the fancy things to impress others and ourselves) and envy (we usually want what others have) dictate your spending habits. Be practical because no matter how much money you spend you will be staring at dark walls in the middle of the night as you hold a screaming baby. You will be constantly changing bedding, blankets, etc. from spit-up, boogers, and diaper blow outs, and you will probably talk about how poor you have become because you have a baby, yet you spent ridiculous amounts of money that didn't need to be spent.

You know what your child will need more than anything? YOUR LOVE!

With that in mind, here's one piece of advice for those of you with bad spending habits or those of you in debt. Do all you can to rid yourselves of those problems before the child comes. The last thing you want is to be unable to provide because you're held captive by your financial struggles.

Survival Tips:

1)Get your finances under control! Not controlling this area of your life could doom your children!

2)Find all your wife's friends and implore them to tell your wife "used" is "best."

3)Encourage your wife's friends to throw a "diaper" shower. You need more diapers and wipes than anything!

4)Stop worrying about money! Anxiety only adds stress to an already stressful situation.

6

TAKE CONTROL OF
YOUR FUTURE!

Once you pass the twenty week mark, reality starts to hit, especially with the upcoming arrival of the first child. Some of my best advice for first-time parents is when you are at this point of pregnancy start talking about what life will look like after the baby is born, because here's the reality: If you do not as a couple start figuring out some of the future realities, good luck! Here are some things to start pondering, to start praying about, and to start crying about (remember, first-time parents are kissing freedom goodbye): (I will try to remain neutral and non-judgmental with my points, but that's not my gift.)

1)Will you put the baby in bed with you? Ummm...I think secretly parents use this as an excuse for a natural birth control. The "tough, strong" answer is "no," but when doing that allows for everyone to get more sleep, your thoughts might change. However, are you going to let an infant control you or are you going to be the person in charge? How you parent now is a good indication of how you parent in the future.

2)Who's getting up with the baby at night? Every couple approaches this differently. I'm keeping my thoughts to myself on this one.

3)Are you going to let the baby cry or always hold him/her? Will you let the baby cry at night, or feed him/her and if so until how old? Figure this one out now because I know too many people who haven't, and they have lost years of their lives due to lack of sleep. Some people say you can't spoil a baby enough, which is true to an extent, but that's probably not a great philosophy to hold to in life. Let me know how that turns out when they're teenagers. Really, this is about doing research, knowing your child, listening to other's advice (trust me, so many of your friends know how to help you, but you're too prideful to listen to their advice), and most importantly learn how to turn down the monitor and close the door! Babies cry; they know the messed up world they're born into, so let them purge their emotions. If you don't, they won't ever get over it and you won't ever get sleep!

4)Are you going to put the child in the nursery at church, work, etc.? One take is to prevent that as long as possible to prevent germs and sickness. However, that's probably just an excuse for people not trusting others. Most professionals say give it 6-8 weeks...very understandable. However, some people view that as 8-10 months. Most people serving/working in those environments have held a lot more babies than you, so really, you're the one who should be questioned. (I say that with love.)

5)Are you going to allow people to babysit? This is a sticky one. Some people won't even let family members babysit, some have no qualms about getting baby sitters, some only let family babysit, and others interview people before allowing them to babysit. Again, all couples have their own ideas with this one, but I think a lot of it relates to #4 as well. Are you not letting others watch your child because you really want to protect him/her, or is it more about you and your insecurities, and often times your lack of faith, and finally your selfishness?

You may not agree with what I write here, but at least give it some thought. When that child pops out and you become a parent, what all of the sudden makes you a parent connoisseur? I'll answer that for you-God. However, who made you a better, more knowledgeable parent than everyone else-no one! I contend that it is more a lack of faith and trust on our parts than anything else. Yes, we should be vigilant with how much to trust others, but we also should remember, especially if you believe in a higher power, that we are not called to worry and to be anxious but quite the opposite. Put some trust in God, put some trust in others, and put some trust in yourself that you can trust others.

Wow, this is getting a little deep so here's one final thought: If you're a helicopter parent at the beginning of your child's life, you will probably be a helicopter parent through time and drive every teacher nuts! (Helicopter parent-parent who enables and who constantly is in the child's "back pocket")

6)Should the woman breastfeed or not? For my personal safety, I will leave this one alone...for the most part. However, I will say that while I do more support the breast-feeding approach, be prepared to deal with the trials of breast-feeding. It doesn't come easy for everyone; it doesn't physically happen for some--no milk production; it can be painful (if the woman has a low pain tolerance=not good); it can make for some awkward public moments and is not exactly car friendly (if the baby is in the car seat, how's the breast feeding going to work...awkward!).

7)If breast-feeding the baby, the parents better prepare for how to feed in public. Some women will be completely embarrassed and isolate themselves from the world every time they feed...like they are diseased or something. Other women have no trouble allowing for all the world to see those milk-enhanced body parts...again making for some awkward moments for those around them. I'm not here to judge which is better (probably a happy medium between the two, including a blanket or "hooter-hider" is best), but make sure you're both on the same page.

8)How much time is the husband going to take off work? While every situation is different, and while financial issues, job flexibility, and birthing complexities can affect time taken from work, make sure this issue is discussed. Many workaholics will take very little to no time off. I'm voting against that because you're just saying your job is more important than your wife and child, even though you won't admit it. On the other hand, some people use all their "vacation" time. While this sounds great, that might not be wise either, because during that first year I guarantee you will be needed at home or want a "break" but you can't get it because you used all that time. Probably most people take a week. That's enough time to help establish some new routines with the baby and to be their together, husband and wife, but it's a short enough time to allow the husband to still feel connected to work. Whatever you decide, be flexible and appreciate the time together.

9)How involved will your parents and in-laws be the first week? Again, while each situation is different, definitely plan for this if you are fortunate to have your parents/in-laws around for help. For us, with our first one we enjoyed having the first week to ourselves. Since we lived away from our parents, Faith's parents drove the 9 hours from Ohio, and mine flew from Colorado to North Carolina for the first couple of days. However, they then left, with my mom and Faith's mom each coming back later for a week at a time while I was back at work. We were able to establish our own routines and protocols (sounds official) without parental interference and judgment. Of course that would never happen! Well, that's how I viewed it. For more insecure women, I would definitely go that route because such women will be questioning/doubting everything anyway and any wrong comment by a "well-intentioned" grandparent (usually grandmother) could severely damage an already fragile psyche. Likewise, since the husband usually will be home that first week, that can make for a crowded house, especially with the stress of having a newborn child. Trust me on this one. Our second child Alexis came one week past the due date, two weeks after my wife's false labor. Yes, my in-laws were in our house for two weeks before the birth...a time I will forever cherish. I wonder why I came home late every day for those two weeks, but I digress.

Survival Tips:

1)Don't wait to plan for that first year until it's too late. Don't procrastinate.

2)Don't be so stubborn that you don't listen to others! However, be discerning. If you spend all day yelling at your kid/s, complaining how draining parenting can be, I'm probably not going to listen to your advice.

3)Face reality now that you cannot, and will not, be able to control all baby situations. Start letting go of control now, before the baby is here.

7

FUTURE GRANDPARENTS

While the role of the grandparents is important once the baby arrives, those future grandparents are often present during pregnancy as well. For many they can offer great advice, support, and money, but they can also add to the stress and anxiety of pregnancy.

First, upon the initial mention of pregnancy, family excitement starts to be a little overwhelming for some. Most future grandparents will be excited and want to do nothing but give you a hug of congratulations. However, be on guard because much like with wedding planning some mothers will want to give the expecting parents all their opinions on what they need for the baby, on how to raise the baby, and on what to do about job situations. Just go with the flow and appreciate the fact you have people who want to be involved in your lives. Vent your frustrations to your spouse, but don't burn bridges with the future babysitters. Plus, you don't want to give anyone ammunition to hold over your head.

On the other hand, some might be completely stunned, especially if the pregnancy comes at a time when the "grandparent/s" don't think you're ready to be a parent. They may be right, but if they start questioning, "Why now?" and "I thought you were waiting longer?" or "Have you even stopped to think about how this will affect work?" rather than start a war with them, do the best to ignore them and to allow everything to sink in. Men, this is easier for us since we can more easily detach ourselves from emotional situations and let things go, but the women might need your support on this one. Plus, regardless of how mad you get at them, they probably aren't going anywhere, and selfishly you want to be in their good graces because you want them buying all the baby stuff so you don't have to.

So, how much should you let them be involved in the whole pregnancy build up? Well, that's going to be different for everyone. I like my space and don't like people telling me what to do, so being away from family made it easier on me in some ways because there wasn't a battle of wills with parents/in-laws. However, I know people who need the extra support and who often times appreciate the extra support. Who wouldn't want the extra help, especially if it means financial help? And, Men, sometimes that extra help and support means that instead of constantly coming to you complaining about feeling fat, bloated, and tired the women can share that experience with their mothers. Likewise, most women don't think men know anything anyway, especially in the pregnancy world. After all, we don't have a punching, kicking being in our stomachs causing us pain, anxiety, restlessness, and exhaustion.

Even though you often are right with your advice, especially since many pregnant women "might" be a little extra emotional, sensitive and irrational with their words and behaviors, it's best to save some stress and to save yourself and to bite your tongue. Let her parents make the mistakes instead of you. Regardless, figure out how much input and space needs to be given now.

If you don't, you will have greater issues to deal with once a child is in the picture.

Survival Tips:

1)Make sure you and your spouse discuss how involved you want your parents. Let them be part of the planning and pregnancy process, but set the precedence during pregnancy. If you don't you will experience unnecessary stress post childbirth.

2)Men, find an escape route when you are "grandma" overwhelmed!

8

COMPLAIN, COMPLAIN, COMPLAIN

In the previous chapter, I alluded to the fact that most women like support. Often times that support is desired in order to receive advice, but often it is for someone just to lend a listening ear for the many complaints and frustrations that are aired during pregnancy. Yes, pregnant woman do like to complain. Men, we just need to suck it up and get over it. Women, I've heard every excuse in the book and know most men would be complete babies if we were pregnant, but there will be complaining and frustrations voiced in almost every conversation a pregnant woman has. Here are a few typical complaints:

1)I keep getting hot flashes at night=The man ends up having covers thrown on and off him all night, so he starts having hot/cold flashes

2)I'm only ____ weeks along. I should still be fitting into my old clothes! I don't have anything to wear!

3)She looks so good. Why can't I look like that? What happened to my hair? It's not straight anymore!

4)Doesn't this type of food sound so good = It will "only" take 20 minutes for the husband to go get it. (Remember, by the time she gets the food she may not want it anymore.)

5)I need 10 pillows, or a body pillow in bed with me.

6)My feet are so swollen!

7)I look like a balloon!

8)I'll never lose this weight!

9)My ring doesn't fit! (Ladies, don't worry, that round stomach will keep other guys away.)

Those are just a few examples of typical complaints and frustrations. And it can get worse. When you and your spouse are around other pregnant women, Men, you need to quickly figure out a game plan to escape the area because when multiple pregnant women are in the same room, watch out! Complaint fest here we come! Are such sessions necessary for women? Sure, but enduring them can be a painful experience for the other party involved.

However, Men, we're great at complaining too. Here are some common man complaints that will hopefully give you a common bond with other men as you make these complaints:

1)I just bought all this food she begged me for and now she doesn't like it!

2)My pants are all too tight because all I do is inhale the food my wife won't eat!

3)How many cravings can a woman have?

4)Hunny, do you remember how we made that baby? Are we ever going to do that again?

5)What an exciting weekend...9:00 bed time for the wife!

6)How much money are we going to spend on maternity clothes?

7)Can you please just borrow clothes?

8)Just because you're tired doesn't mean I'm tired.

In a perfect world, we wouldn't complain, and we would be totally understanding, forgiving, and supportive of our spouses in all situations. Unfortunately, we're not perfect (yes, shocking for some of you), so the whole pregnancy stage will be difficult. Just remember that most of what you're thinking should stay in your thoughts and not be heard, especially by your wife, and realize that you will get your spouse back.

Survival Tips:

1)No matter how difficult it will be, just be a listening ear to your wife. We hate to admit it, but we really can't relate to what they're experiencing.

2)Don't add to the complaining. Complaining just leads to ungratefulness, and it makes for too many unhappy moments in the home.

9

TO WORK OR NOT TO WORK

As you progress through the pregnancy stages, many harsh realities set in, and one of the most difficult decisions many parents are forced to make is that of who works, who doesn't work, and how much should people work. As with all the other great parenting decisions you must make, this is not to be taken lightly and again can cause wars in your marriage and families. For the sake of protecting "my life," I'm going to delicately tread waters on this one, but the issue must be addressed.

The following charts show basic pros and cons of each decision:

	Pros	**Cons**
Working	-Actually have money to buy all the new baby necessities (food, diapers, etc.) -Able to interact with people who can respond to you with actual words (however, this can be bad depending on whom you work with) -Gives variety to your day -Can allow you to more appreciate the time you do have with your child/children -Adds normalcy to life - back to previous routine	-Minimize the time you have with your child -Often gives other authority figures more influences, or at least a shared influence, over your child's life. -Constantly worried about child's health, safety, etc. -Separation anxiety, for both child and mother -Daycare sucks away your money -Say hello to germs if child is in daycare with other children = hello work sick-days -Bring home a lot of the stresses from the job and don't have the appropriate energy to give to the child -Who cooks food and does laundry?

	Pros	Cons
Staying Home	-Allows the parent to raise the child instead of sharing that with others -Maximizes parental influence in the child's life -Can give purpose to people not satisfied with their work/material lives -Provides time to interact with other moms -Can minimize the morning stress of getting out the door for work -Allows time for parent involvement in pre-school/school -More time to make dinner and do laundry! -Not ashamed to admit it-I sometimes come home to a lawn mowed by my wife!	-Dad comes home and wants a few minutes to recover from day, and Mom wants off "child" duty, which means tension -If mom does not leave house much during day, she wants to talk husband's ear off -Again, more tension -Especially at the beginning, moms feel isolated and lack purpose as now their days are focused on only one person, the child -No MONEY!

Regardless of the decision you make, make sure it's not due to the judgment you feel from others. The decision should be between the spouses. Hey, you could reverse roles and have the dad stay at home while the wife works. No matter what happens, here's my simple-minded advice for the adjustment:

1) Avoid bringing work home. As a teacher, I know how notorious teachers are for bringing work home. Forget it! Manage your time at work better. If one spouse has been home all day, you owe it to him/her to focus on the family and to give that spouse a break when you're home. If you both work, it doesn't take a genius to figure out the work at home equals more home stress.

2) Men, get over your antiquated (that means "old") ways and help in the kitchen, help with laundry, or do some cleaning. What! How can that be? I'll tell you how. If you're both working, how weak are we men admitting we are if we expect our wives to do all of that home work on top of working. And, if the wife is home during the day, she is spending time with your child, teaching and instructing him/her, so don't expect all that other stuff to be done. If she works around the house all

day, ignoring your child, she might as well get a job that pays.

Survival Tips:

1)Stop making your life about how much money you make. Do you both work because you love working and love your work, or is it strictly based on you wanting to maintain a certain standard of living?

2)Know that whatever choice you make, there will be great change in your lives!

10

HOME STRETCH

As you approach those final days and weeks, know that you're going from one new difficult, challenging, exciting, fun stage to another that is far greater than what you just experienced. However, before the big day nears, you better address a few final points.

1)Should you take all those birthing classes? This is all personal opinion. Through our four pregnancies, we took "0" classes. It's called the Internet! However, we know others who were greatly put at ease by the classes. Every couple approaches life differently, and especially if one of you is insecure or if pregnancy is rocking your world, visit some classes. You will learn something and realize others are in your same shoes.

2)When should you pack your "hospital" bag?
Pack sooner rather than later. Our first child came two weeks early, our second came a week late, the third was on the due date, and the fourth was a week early. Make sure you pack the necessities like toiletries, comfortable slip-on shoes or slippers, and warm clothes, even if it's the middle of summer. My hospital experience is that it is much cooler in the hospital than it is outside. No matter what, make sure your wife is packed. When she's in the middle of contractions, she just cares about how much time is in between each one. I actually don't think I packed until it was time to go, but do as I say not as I do. Don't add more stress than already exists.

3)Who will be in the delivery room besides you and the medical team?
First of all, suck it up and be in the room with your wife! She's experiencing way worse than you, so be there for her. And, that's all I would suggest be there. There will be enough doctors and nurses flying around the room.

4)Most importantly, make sure your wife has friends with whom she can experience this whole new baby world. Men, you don't want to be the only one she can lean on. It's not healthy for either one of you!

For Women

Friends are a great asset when it comes to baby showers, maternity clothing, and baby clothes because they so often want to help, often times buying things you might not otherwise buy. However, that's just a surface bonus of friendship; although, I'm a big fan of other people buying baby things for the many soon-to-be "poor" parents. Friendships should go much deeper, which was made ever more clear when our family made our first voyage back to our old stomping grounds in North Carolina. In our six days there, we managed to see many people who were part of our lives for the past eight years. Before we headed home, we closed out the NC portion of the trip with a big get together with all the mom's and kids that were part of a women's Bible study over our sons first six years of life. So, minus one or two kids who were in school, there were 20 kids running around the house with their mothers watching. I reference that time together because those ladies have gone through pregnancy, birth, and child rearing together. They have spent countless hours on the phone, email, social media, and at one another's homes, giving advice to and spending time with one another. I know too many mothers who don't have that so all they do is sit on the computer surfing the Internet for advice or get on social media sites, posting their questions to all those "Social Media" friends. While it might sound like I'm judging you for using the Internet to solve your problems, I'm not, but nothing can replace the interactions people have with more "real" friends.

You need people to call you up to check on your sanity when your husband is out of town and you're alone with the wonderful, crazy kids. You need friends to email you those awesome coupon deals. You need people to spend time with, giving your children opportunities to play with others. You need those friends to be there for the struggles with miscarriages, for the constant battle with discipline of your children, for the breast feeding support (husbands can only give so much support here), and for those dinner get-aways with friends to escape the craziness of parenthood.

So, what do you need to do? If you don't have that friend support, I strongly encourage you to stop being afraid, get outside of your bubble, and reach out to others. When you do that, others will reach out to you. Whether you have children or are in that pregnancy phase, value those friends you have and seek to establish those friendships you, and others, need.

For Men

Men, your job is a lot easier. Be there for your wife and be the rock and pillar she needs in times of struggle. Whatever you do, be careful about giving advice (kind of ironic since I just wrote three paragraphs giving women advice) because you will find yourself digging out of huge holes if you always try to solve her problems. If your wife is pregnant and you realize she is in a place where she does not have many female friends and/or people to lean on, get over yourself and help her get connected. Church is a great place to start! I really don't know too many other *opportunities where a pregnant women can jump in and find a group of friends. She's not drinking, so she's not at the bar. She's probably not exercising too much so the gym is out. Maybe she likes to knit or crochet (especially if she's in the Midwest), work on the computer, scrapbook, etc. Whatever you do, help her find common ground with others, especially if your wife is staying at home and will not have the social interaction the work environment gives. Above all else, encourage her and pray for her!*

Survival Tips:

1)Men, pregnancy can really suck, so no matter what be supportive of your wife.

2)Ladies, recognize how we struggle with our lives changing so please give us our space during the pregnancy experience, especially the last few weeks, to relish in the final moments of no parenting responsibilities.

3)Enjoy the ride because one of the greatest journeys of life is about to begin!

ABOUT THE AUTHOR

Matt Perkins has taught English in and worked in the public school system for over eleven years. He and his wife, Faith, have four children: Isaiah, Alexis, Audrey, and Timothy. Matt grew up in Colorado, he and Faith spent their first eight years of marriage in North Carolina, and now they live in Ohio.

While he has spent his adult life educating and coaching students, Matt has always felt that few books are written at an accessible, and enjoyable, level for all male readers. It's time all men can appreciate and enjoy reading! What About the Man?

Made in the USA
San Bernardino, CA
21 December 2014